Samhain

and other poems in Irish Metres of the
Eighth to the Sixteenth Centuries

ROBIN SKELTON

Samhain

and other poems in Irish Metres of the
Eighth to the Sixteenth Centuries

SALMON POETRY

First published in 1994 by
Salmon Publishing Ltd,
A division of Poolbeg Enterprises Ltd,
Knocksedan House,
123 Baldoyle Industrial Estate,
Dublin 13, Ireland

The moral right of the author has been asserted.

The publishers gratefully acknowledge the support of An Comhairle
Ealaíon/The Arts Council and the Arts Council of Northern Ireland

A catalogue record for this book is available from the British Library.

ISBN 1 897648 13 8

Cover illustration "A Letter for Rembrant" by John Kelly, Mixed media on
paper, from The Collection of the Arts Council/An Chomhairle Ealaíon
Back cover photograph by James Tuohy
Cover design by Poolbeg Group Services Ltd
Set by Poolbeg Group Services Ltd in Palatino 11/15
Printed by Colour Books, Baldoyle Industrial Estate, Dublin 13.

To the living memory of

a printer of brilliance,
a publisher of genius,
the guide and guardian of
so many Irish poets
writers and artists,
and a friend.

Poetry

An Irish Gathering (1964)
An Irish Album (1969)
Remembering Synge (1971)

Criticism

The Writings of J M Synge (1971)
Celtic Contraries (1990)

Editions

J M Synge: Translations (1961)
J M Synge: Four Plays and the Aran Islands (1962)
J M Synge: Collected Poems (1962)
J M Synge: Riders to the Sea (1969)
Synge / Petrarch (1971)
The Collected Plays of Jack B Yeats (1971)
The Selected Writings of Jack B Yeats (1991)

Anthologies

Six Irish Poets (1962)

Contents

From the sixth to the fourteenth centuries the lyric poets of the British Isles appear to have been almost wholly Irish or Welsh. It was not until after the death of Chaucer in 1400 that the poets of England produced those wonderful Middle English Lyrics we admire and are taught in Universities. We are not, most of us, taught the much more complex lyrics of the Welsh and the Irish/Scots (for the literary Gaelic of this period was common to both Ireland and Scotland). In the Renaissance English poets imported verse forms and metres from the continent of Europe, but, with a couple of exceptions, failed to note the wealth of formal artistry even closer at hand. Indeed, so far as I am aware, nobody has seriously attempted to carry the Irish formulae over into English, though Welsh has been more often tackled.

One reason for this may be that the metrics of Irish lyric are so complex and sophisticated that they are inclined to put would-be imitators off. A number of Irish scholars went on record as calling them difficult, regarding the *deibide* (or *deibhidhe*) as '*The hardest thing under the sun*' (O'Molloy), and '*The most difficult and scientific of all the classical forms of verse*' (Eleanor Hull). These views were ridiculed by Osborn Bergin, but he was a master of verse craft and composed verse (if not poetry) not only in Irish but also in Latin, Greek, Sanskrit and Arabic as well as English.

I have myself composed poems in these Irish

metres for several reasons. Firstly, I was simply curious as to whether or not these forms could be used in English, and how working within them would affect both my style and my thinking. Secondly, having already tackled the metres of Wales, I wished to complete my exploration of the verse of my Celtic ancestors. Thirdly, I fell in love with the beautiful complexities, the possibilities of harmony, and the grace of these forms and that was, perhaps, the strongest compulsion of all.

Once upon a time, at a not absolutely sober gathering of Irish poets and writers, I was elected an *Honorary Irish Poet*. The election, I fear, had no validity, but perhaps in this book I have moved a small step towards justifying the honour.

Robin Skelton

Victoria
British Columbia

Two in a Garden

(Áe Freslige)

Lovers, we lie wondering
why our amorous leisure's
marred by spectres blundering
through our pastoral pleasures

under trees' tranquillity
blossoming boughs above us,
whispering futility
and names of other lovers.

Spring Sprung

(Brecchairdne)

Joyful and wanton
Spring is awakening;
green spears are quivering
and buds boldly swelling.

Sharing its graceful
spread petals the golden
primrose is gleaming
all over the garden.

Birth is beginning;
the daffodils, bouncing
their clusters of belfries,
are pealing, rejoicing.

Birds are attempting
the rituals of nesting
with twigs and straws, tatters
and scraps they are testing.

Life is in riot,
roaring, unreasoning;
restless, irrational
I find myself writing

verses that wonder
what happens to winter,
then wonder why ever
they bother to wonder

for this is Springtime
and no time for questions
on serious subjects
but for the glad season's

singing and dancing,
for laughter and playful
games of the goddess,
wanton and joyful.

The Wilderness
(Casbairdne)

Mysteries are obstacles
to the strictly sensible,
wilderness ridiculous
and absurdly bountiful,

all of it untidiness,
such useless territories
only good for infantile
fancies and effronteries,

but Earth's irresponsible,
shapes unstable histories,
and retains love's wilderness
as mankind its mysteries.

Observation

(Cethramtu rannaigechta móire)

Oceans rise,
forests fall;
Time, watching,
sees it all.

Time, watching,
sees the rocks
break under
earthquake shocks,

sees rivers
dry to stone,
each creature
shrunk to bone,

roots withered
black as grain,
men, women
eating pain,

humankind
at an end.
Time, watching,
can't pretend

grief, shock; in
pale clear eyes
oceans fall,
forests rise.

Time Past

(Cró cumaisc etir casbairdni ocus lethrannaigecht)

Time is a long forgetting
and a drifting mist
that softens our regretting,
veils the loves we've kissed,

and reshapes our emotions
so we are not hurt
by long ago devotions
that destroyed the heart.

Dismissing as delusions
shames our nights recall,
it simplifies confusions
but lets the curtain fall

on much we would remember
if we only could—
something about December,
something in a wood,

his name, her name, possessions
that are lost to view;
now even our confessions
can't be wholly true.

Time past is a condition
of our being here,

and if that means omission
of delight or fear,

it means, too, expectation
and new hills to climb
preserved from hesitation
by forgetful Time.

The Wood at Evening

(Dechnad Mór)

Walking the wood at day's end,
sensing in every sound
wandering words of the wind
hinting at futures to find,

I think of the way a woman
answers a glance with a glance,
scanning farther than reason,
teaching her music to man,

and touch a tree in wonder,
pondering ways that wisdom
comes from bewitching women,
from winds in trees while walking.

Beehive Huts, West Kerry
For John Montague

(Dechnad cummaisc)

Behind the farmyard the beehives,
grey stone dwellings
for dark tribes and their children
wildly tumbling

the green slopes edging the ocean
seem to huddle
in the mist as if they're hiding,
tired of muddles

we have made, just as we've also
marred and hindered
worship in the sacred places
of past kindred

whose simplicities of wisdom
our days disdain,
calling these stone houses hovels,
yet they remain

reminders of how time changes
almost nothing
essential; we still are mortal,
fragile, living

however we can in countries
we've not designed,
dreaming we may, death-deceiving,
leave truths behind.

Young
For Xan

(Deibide)

Seeing you smile, I despair
ever of watching over
you in your long years ahead
for deadly Time's defeated

many more worthy than I
and I know none less likely
now to find favour with fate,
having no mite of merit.

Yet you yourself, if you wish
and care, could make me flourish;
imagine me young once more
and Time, turning hopes over,

will grant long life, for no-one
could rule out a revision
from one so wise and so young,
seeing the smile I'm seeing.

For a Newborn God-Daughter

(Deibide baise fri tóin)

Here, alone,
I think of the vast unknown
enclosed in your wrinkled kissed
fist

that, intent
upon heaven's now lost extent,
fumbles to find and to keep
sleep.

By the Lake

(Deibide Guilbnech)

Beyond the quivering reeds
a flicker of brightness leads
the watcher upon the shore
to repudiate earth-lore,

become a breath on the lake,
a ripple, a drifting flake,
a speck, a reflected white
wool cloud, wet-bright as the light,

not man at all, but a part
of the water's beating heart
and Time's beginning, in bond
to this one dawn and beyond.

The Visitant
For Brigid

(Debide guilbnech dialtach)

Arms raised to praise the earth
for stirrings of coming birth
I find I am holding my breath
in case I should embrace death.

But I am feeling the leap
and kick of a soul from sleep,
the lunge and twitch of a shape
about to achieve escape

with a vital delightful zest
that time will put to the test
from the naked squalling start,
and now, here, under her heart

I know there are joys and tears,
miracles, wonders, fears,
a future of storms and calms,
mankind new-born in her arms.

Samhain
For Alison

(Droigneach)

Mystery attends the year when Earth confesses
an uncontrollable need of celebration
and each leaf in the Autumn orchard expresses
in ochre and bronze and crimson the conflagration

needed now the seasons are nearing transition,
the fire that is power and pride and supervenes
whenever the slowing sun threatens inanition,
pallid and shadowy over the evergreens

that still spire upwards, needles gaunt, unchanging,
remote, it would seem, from the earth's
                              predicament.
There comes a time in the year when, rearranging
summer memories, colours rustling, resplendent,

the crisp dry leaves call out to us and, responding,
we build a fire of the broken and dismembered
fragments of earthly suffering and, extending
hands to the dead who are, in this blaze,
                              remembered,

celebrate the riches we've known, the profusion,
the births, the deaths, the ever changing history,
finding in fire a vision beyond illusion,
welcoming the holiness and the mystery.

Connemara
For Susan Musgrave

(Lethrannaigecht Mór)

Connemara, green
blest country of stone
where the sea-mists shine
a light all their own,

I am with you still;
though a long time stray
you must feel me stand
where the dolmens pray

in their rain-soft veils
to the wise ones above
the huddled thatched roofs,
the round hills we love,

the silver white strands,
the mounds of brown weed,
the tides lapping land
for all of us need

to stand where we can
and speak to those gone
beyond the soft green
and the grey scattered stone.

Outcrop

For Margaret Snow

(Rannaigecht)

Land under me, watching the stars,
I stroll the high field and stand
upon moss-covered granite,
the ancient grain of the land.

On bedrock here, I return
to the pulse of this old stone
under me, earth's origin
within the wind and the rain

abrading and changing all,
creating gravel and loam,
cutting the canyon's channel,
providing the runnels with room

hugely to deepen and swell
till, rivers, they meet the sea
that, moving to the moon-pulse,
evolved all the life to be.

Or so, here, under the stars
I tell myself as I stand
on the moss-covered granite,
the signature of the land.

Against Learning

(Rannaigecht bec)

No learning
can answer the tides turning
under the moon or reply
to the cry of the sun burning,

or ever
understand any lover
trapped in the pains of pleasure,
all mind-made measures over,

for passion
is one with the tides' action,
the sun's heat, the moon's control;
thus all souls, in their fashion

wise, discerning,
praise scholarship for its turning
to vision and to insight,
sunlit and moonlit learning.

The Making of Music

(Rannaigecht Bheag)

Piping men thought that music
was taken from a feather
of sly Eros by magic
to trick and tease the hearer

with sounds for dancing lovers,
enlivening the passions,
contriving sentimental
lies to spur seductions.

I'm not of this opinion,
preferring to consider
our music wholly sea-born,
the moon our one composer,

except, of course, for certain
tuneful fantasies stepping
lightly around our garden,
for there I hear Pan piping.

Crepuscule
For Sylvia

(Rannaigecht gairit)

Nearing night
as day is a dying light
and we walk our island shore
the ripples of foam are bright.

Twilight brings
that brightness to many things,
suffusing the hours we spend
as we end our wanderings

blessed by white
walled rooms where today I write
of loving and living here
contentedly nearing night.

The Names

(Rannaigecht Mór)

Air me your favourite name,
one you would give to a stone
you felt had a pulse of flame
untamed by the known, alone

there on the earth at your feet,
or tell me the name you'd give
to the first child that you meet
in the street where lovers live,

or the one you long to write
on vellum to see it shine
with elegance and delight,
bright as the sacred sign

on gospels in bishops' courts,
or tell me the name you share
with nothing in human thoughts,
but with water, earth, fire, air.

Rowan

(Rinnard)

Reason can not explain
how the Autumn rowan
history thought holy
found its vivid crimson.

Legends have their answers,
Christian and Pagan;
they are only stories
setting out a pattern

suitable for children
playing in the garden.
I find myself driven
to an older version,

feel those berries risen
from a burning brightness
in the heart of silence
where I see the goddess

standing like a rowan
crowned by more than crimson,
giving man a present
of her own heart's reason.

Alba

(Rinnard Tri-nard)

Leaving her still sleeping
underneath the covers
safe from winter's cramping
is usual for lovers

who discover pleasure
in precluding grieving
and a kind of grandeur
in a well-planned leaving.

Intermission

(Seadna)

Gone to lie in leaf-lit dapple,
drowsing in the summer sun,
sky is simply a blue bubble,
mind a mummer babbling on.

Crows caw no concern or worry;
wildfowl float serenely by;
nothing here's prepared to hurry;
no-one needs to probe or pry.

Even bees sieze the occasion,
crawling slowly round warm blooms,
revelling in languid leisure;
spiders cease to work their looms.

Yet the fretful world is waiting
worriedly to hurry on
and Fall's bell will soon be sounding,
summer pleasure spurned and gone.

Pike
For Diane Keating

(Seadna Mór)

Reasoning beside the river
bridge, I sense his position,
an old one ageless in wisdom,
wanton with erudition,

lurking as knowledge is lurking
always, lost and forgotten,
crippled by history's burden,
great books burned or forbidden.

Learning is always relearning;
loss is always happening;
a pike haunts every river,
hiding from our reasoning.

Memories

(Snám súad)

Memories,
moon-led seas,
sliding tides,
uncover
early days,
time-drowned ways,
and appraise
each lover,

pointing out
here a doubt,
there a trust,
a fashion,
dwelling on
lusts long gone
and that one
true passion

no-one knew
although you,
dazzled by
its glory,
ached to tell
the miracle,
the pinnacle
of story

that now seems
elsewhere's dreams
and holds no
sorceries,
she a whore,
he a bore;
few adore
memories.

Orchard Incident

(Snéd-bairdne)

Shaking the tatter-leaved branches
in the garden
to bring down the withered apples,
scarred and hardened

by weathers of wet wild autumn,
and then stooping
to tangled grass where they've hidden,
grasping, groping,

gathering this last hurt harvest,
I'm unmaking
apple dreams, their night's daybreaker
waking, shaking.

The Toys
(Trëochair)

Day ended,
I look back and remember
the toys nobody mended.

Wheels shattered,
heads cracked, lead men dismembered,
parts lost, none of it mattered.

My grieving
was childish and natural,
but quite soon I'd be leaving

home for all
those boarding school solitudes,
the massed prayers, the football,

and learning
myself, my own sensations;
there could be no returning

though haunted
sometimes by sad disturbing
thoughts of toys that I'd wanted

to possess
always, loyal, devoted,
for they were the happiness,

the sorrow,
the friends and companions
of each day, each tomorrow.

Day ended,
I look back and remember
the toys nobody mended.

On the Moor
For Jane Urquhart

(Trian Rannaigechta móire)

A lone pleasure's
wandering where
purple heather,
haunting air,

appears to move
within the eye
as if a mode
of memory,

a kind of dream
that is a past
we never knew
and never lost

but keep within
the marrow bone
and feel it when
we walk alone.

Playing the Game
(Murphy 18)

Anyone rhymed it:
Give us a penny
(the game that summer)
I have not any.

Playtime is over
maybe for ever.
Now it is *Give me*
a new young lover,

knowing the answer
before it's spoken.
Dreaming is over,
the mirror broken,

one hope remaining,
last of the many:
Give me a reason.
I have not any.

The Well

(Murphy 8)

I at wellhead,
leaning over,
   see wet gold;
it shines, shaking
in the water;
   I've been told

there is magic
in this vision
   of the sun;
trembling, spinning
in the darkness,
   it means one

could find fortune
here by wishing
   the right way,
gain a treasure
or a lover.
   Some folk say

this is rubbish,
but some others
   won't deny
the old story;
seeking glory,
   nor will I.

At Knocknarea
I. M. Robert Speaight

(Murphy 12)

Still beneath Knocknarea,
watching my friend climb
to the cairn, days fell away;
we escaped from Time,

no longer friends at all
but part of a dream
mankind knows perpetual
as willow and stream,

his tread inscribing the mound
with letters to say
'Man only finds the long found,
prays how ages pray.

Whether or not you climb high
or remain below
you breathe in the distant sky,
grow as grasses grow,

but to some is there given,
and suddenly, light
breaking from earth or heaven.'
Sharp etched on my sight,

smaller and smaller he grew.
Then he stood alone
beside great Maeve and I knew
he communed with stone

for an infinite moment.
Returned down the hill,
he took my hand; the current
sustained him still.

Appendix: The Metrics

Metrics

Irish/Scots poetry from the eighth to the sixteenth centuries and later was syllabic and rhymed. In presenting the formulae of these forms I have placed the required number of syllables in the last word of the line in brackets. The rhymes are indicated conventionally by letters of the alphabet. Internal (or aicill) rhymes are indicated separately.

Rhyming in Irish/Scots was not as strict as that of some other cultures. Indeed, one might state that we would call some Irish rhyming simply consonance, or even assonance. 'Chiming' might be a better word than 'rhyming' in some instances. In making these poems I have been as approximate in chiming as many Irish poets before me.

A general rule that applies to Irish forms is that the poem should end with the syllable or word with which it began. In practice this sometimes meant that the word or syllable were merely repeated within the last line. These *dunadh* endings are more frequent in some forms than in others and not all poems have this characteristic. The poems in this collection vary in this regard. The majority have *dunadh* endings but in some instances the complete first line is repeated or the second rather than the first word. Once the *dunadh* ending is entirely omitted.

I have taken these forms from a number of sources, but must acknowledge particularly the work of Gerard Murphy and his collection, *Early Irish Lyrics* (The

Clarendon Press 1956). I have accepted his labelling of forms whenever possible and those unnamed forms he presented I have given the name Murphy followed by the number of the poem utilising the form in his collection.

Áe Freislighe

Syllables	7(3)	7(2)	7(3)	7(2)
Endrhymes	a	b	a	b

Breccbairdne

Syllables	5(2)	6(2)	6(2)	6(2)
Endrhymes	a	b	c	b

All the end words consonate.

Casbairdne

Syllables	7(3)	7(3)	7(3)	7(3)
Endrhymes	a	b	c	b

The endwords *a* and *c* are in consonance with the *b* word. The final syllable of line 4 alliterates with the stressed syllable preceding it. The endwords of lines 1 and 3 rhyme with words in the middle of lines 2 and 4 respectively.

Cethramtu rannaigechta moire

Syllables	3(1)	3(1)	3(1)	3(1)
Endrhymes	a	b	c	b

Cró cumaisc etir casbairdni ocus lethrannaigecht

Syllables	7(3)	5(1)	7(3)	5(1)
Endrhymes	a	b	a	b

The third line may sometimes end with a disyllabic word that rhymes into the middle of the following line. This is called an *aicill* rhyme.

Deachnadh Mór

Syllables	8(2)	6(2)	8(2)	6(2)
Endrhymes	a	b	a	b

The rhymes are, in fact, consonance. The first two lines rhyme with each other in the body of the lines, as do the second two lines; in the first two lines the rhyme may be no more than consonance, but in the second two it must be true rhyme. The last word of the third line rhymes with one in the middle of the fourth line. Each line should contain two words that alliterate with each other.

Dechnad cummaisc

Syllables	8(2)	4(2)	8(2)	4(2)
Endrhymes	a	b	c	b

The last word of line 3 rhymes into the middle of line 4 (*Aicill* rhyme).

Deibide or Deibhidhe

Syllables	7	7	7	7
Endrhymes	a	a	b	b

The first and third lines end with stressed syllables, the second and fourth lines with unstressed ones. The last word of the stanza alliterates with the preceding stressed word. The last word of the third line rhymes with a word in the middle of the line following. The rhyming of a stressed with an unstressed syllable is referred to as *Deibide* rhyme.

Deibide baise fri tóin

Syllables	3(2)	7(2)	7(1)	1(1)
Endrhymes	a	a	b	b

Deibide Guilbnech

Syllables	7	7	7	7
Endrhymes	a	a	b	b

In this variation of the *Deibide* formula all the endrhymes are stressed. There is alliteration and internal rhyme as in *Deibide*.

Debide guilbnech dialtach

Syllables	7(1)	7(1)	7(1)	7(1)
Endrhymes	a	a	b	b

All the endwords consonate.

Droighneach

Syllables	9-13(3)	9-13(3)	9-13(3)	9-13(3)
Endrhymes	a	b	a	b

A stanza may be composed of several quatrains if so desired.

Lethrannaigecht Mór

Syllables	5(1)	5(1)	5(1)	5(1)
Endrhymes	a	b	c	b

If the last word of the third line does not rhyme into the middle of the fourth line, then the *a* and *c* words should consonate with the *b* word. This is an early rule. Later the consonantal linking was replaced by *aicill* rhyme. The first two lines are linked by assonance within the lines. This device is called *amus*.

Rannaigecht

Syllables	7(1)	7(1)	7(2)	7(1)
Endrhymes	a	b	c	b

There is *aicill* rhyme in lines 3 and 4 and sometimes in lines 1 and 2. The final words of lines 1, 2 and 4 consonate.

Rannaigecht bec

Syllables	3(2)	7(2)	7(2)	7(2)
Endrhymes	a	a	b	a

The final word of the third line has an *aicill* rhyme with the middle of the fourth. There is a variant form in which we find:

Endrhymes	a	b	a	b

The end words of lines three and four may alliterate.

Rannaigheacht Bheag

Syllables	7(2)	7(2)	7(2)	7(2)
Endrhymes	a	b	a	b

The rhyming is, in fact, consonance rather than true rhyme. Line 3 has an *aicill* rhyme with line 4 and the final word of line 4 alliterates with the word immediately preceding it.

Rannaigheacht Ghairid

Syllables	3(1)	7(1)	7(1)	7(1)
Endrhymes	a	a	b	a

The last word of the third line has an aicill rhyme into the middle of the line following.

Rannaigheacht Mór

Syllables	7(1)	7(1)	7(1)	7(1)
Endrhymes	a	b	a	b

The rhyming is, in fact, consonance. The final word of line 3 has an *aicill* rhyme with the middle of line 4 and the last word of line 4 alliterates with the preceding word.

Rinnard

Syllables	6(2)	6(2)	6(2)	6(2)
Endrhymes	a	b	c	b

The *a* and *c* words consonate with *b*. There is an *aicill* rhyme between lines 3 and 4.

Rionnaird Tri-nard

Syllables	6(2)	6(2)	6(2)	6(2)
Endrhymes	a	b	c	b

Line 3 consonates with lines 2 and 4. The last syllable of the first line alliterates with the first stressed syllable of the second. The last words of lines 2 and 3 rhyme into the middle of lines 3 and 4 respectively.

Seadna

Syllables	8(2)	7(1)	8(2)	7(1)
Endrhymes	a	b	c	b

The last word of the first line alliterates with the first stressed word of the line following. The third line rhymes with the stressed word immediately preceding the last word of the stanza, and the last word of the stanza alliterates with both these words.

Seadna Mór

Syllables	8(2)	7(3)	8(2)	7(3)
Endrhymes	a	b	c	b

Apart from the altered organisation of the syllables *Seadna Mór* is identical with *Seadna*.

Setna Mór

Syllables	8(2)	7(3)	8(2)	7(3)
Endrhymes	a	b	c	b

The final word of the third line rhymes into the middle of the fourth.

Snám súad

Syllables	3(1)	3(1)	3(1)	3(3)	3(1)	3(1)	3(1)	3(3)
Endrhymes	a	a	b	c	d	d	d	c

The *a* rhymes may be imperfect. Lines 2 and 3 are lined by consonance. The lines 3 and4, 6 and 7, 4 and 4 and 7 are linked by alliteration. The 7th line contains alliteration.

Snéd-bairdne

Syllables	8(2)	4(2)	8(2)	4(2)
Endrhymes	a	b	c	b

In line 4 every stressed word must rhyme. The *a* and *c* end words consonate with the *b* word.

Trëochair

Syllables	3(2)	7(3)	7(2)
Endrhymes	a	b	a

There is frequent alliteration.

Trian Rannaigechta Moire

Syllables	4(1)	4(1)	4(1)	4(1)
Endrhymes	a	b	c	b

All the end words consonate. There is *aicill* rhyme between the third and fourth lines.

Unnamed Metre (Murphy 18)

Syllables	5(2)	5(2)	5(2)	5(2)
Endrhymes	a	b	a	b

The *b* rhymes are constant, but the *a* rhymes may be either imperfect or omitted. Occasion *aicill* rhyme occurs between lines 1 and 4.

UNN

Unnamed Metre. (Murphy 8)

Syllables	4(2)	4(2)	3(1)	4(2)	4(2)	3(1)
Endrhymes	a	b	c	d	e	c

Unnamed Metre.(Murphy 12)

Syllables	7 (1, 2 or 3)	5(1)	7 (1, 2 or 3)	5(1)
Endrhymes	a	b	a	b

The endword of line 3 rhymes into the middle of line 4 (*Aicill* rhyme). The *a* rhymes are permitted to be approximate.